## Enriching Faith

# LESSONS AND ACTIVITIES ON PRAYER

CATHERINE STEWART

TWENTY-THIRD PUBLICATIONS
twentythirdpublications.com

TWENTY-THIRD PUBLICATIONS
A Division of Bayard
One Montauk Avenue, Suite 200
New London, CT 06320
(860) 437-3012 or (800) 321-0411
www.twentythirdpublications.com

Second Printing 2016

Copyright ©2014 Catherine Stewart.
Permission is given to reproduce the activity pages in this book as needed for non-commercial use in schools and parish religious education programs. Otherwise, no part of this publication may be reproduced in any manner without prior written permission of the publisher. Write to the Permissions Editor.

ISBN: 978-1-58595-947-1
Library of Congress Control Number: 2013952208
Printed in the U.S.A.

# CONTENTS

Introduction     5

## traditional prayer

| | | |
|---|---|---|
| 1 | SIGN OF THE CROSS | 6 |
| 2 | THE OUR FATHER | 6 |
| 3 | THE GLORY BE | 14 |
| 4 | THE HAIL MARY | 18 |
| 5 | GUARDIAN ANGEL PRAYER | 22 |
| 6 | APOSTLE'S CREED | 28 |
| 7 | ACT OF CONTRITION | 30 |
| 8 | MEAL PRAYER | 32 |

## forms of prayer

| | | |
|---|---|---|
| 9 | INTERCESSION | 36 |
| 10 | CONTRITION | 40 |
| 11 | BLESSING | 44 |
| 12 | PRAISE | 44 |
| 13 | THANKSGIVING | 44 |

## meditative prayer

| | | |
|---|---|---|
| 14 | IMAGINATIVE PRAYERS | 55 |
| 15 | LECTIO DIVINA | 59 |
| 16 | ART AS PRAYER | 63 |

# ACKNOWLEDGMENTS

Writing a book is a mysterious journey that begins with a single word. Many wonderful people walked beside me as I discovered ways to engage children in the wonder of prayer and meditative practices. I am especially grateful for the blessings received from the following:

- Father Mark Osterhaus, a good friend of mine, who encouraged me to write this second book. He continues to inspire me as he connects the Word to ordinary, everyday life. When I was at a loss for words, he helped me find just the right words deep within me.
- Rosanne Coffey, who edited the book and gave wonderful suggestions for fine-tuning the directions; I always looked forward to our conversations, and she encouraged my creativity whenever I was excited about a new idea. Rosanne has become a real friend!
- Jeff McCall, who did the layout of this book. I know all of us appreciate the user-friendly pages!
- Lindsey Leach, a Blackburn College student and a whiz at the computer; she generated templates, resizing or changing them as needed, so the students can use them easily.
- Allison Bruss, a Blackburn College student, who created the truth-telling and liar tongue templates.
- Dominican Sisters of Springfield, Illinois, who once again supported me with their belief in this project, their encouraging words, resources, and assistance in marketing!
- My family, who are amazed that I can "grow books from deep within me" the way they can grow corn and soybeans!
- My colleagues at Blackburn College who "know the writing look" and quickly back out of my office so as not to disturb me, but later inquire as to how the book is coming along and willingly read first drafts with a careful eye.
- Everyone at Twenty-Third Publications, who once again helped me feel very comfortable with the process.

# INTRODUCTION

Our lives are filled with variety. We have, for example, a variety of foods to eat and a variety of clothes to wear. All of these varieties and many more meet the various needs we have.

Our spiritual life reflects our physical life. We need a variety of prayers and practices in order to meet the needs of our souls. Traditional prayers, spontaneous prayers, meditative practices, and creative prayers meet our different needs as we set aside time to talk with God. All of us have our favorite prayers for different occasions. Some of my friends enjoy praying the Hail Mary over and over whenever there is a crisis. Others pray the Angel of God prayer whenever they feel a need to be safe. Some take a blanket and a Bible and head outside on a warm summer day to rest and relax in God's arms as they imagine themselves in one of the Scripture stories. At other times, the soul needs to create, for we are made in the image and likeness of our Creator; therefore, we hear a call to pray using art. Prayer is our way of communicating with God, who waits and longs for our love.

This book can be used in a variety of ways. Catechists and Catholic schoolteachers can use it as they review or teach the traditional prayers for the first time. Students will find the activities engaging and easy to accomplish. An intergenerational prayer evening can be planned, and each of the prayer experiences can be an individual station. All involved can review the traditional prayers and experience newer prayer practices. Grandparents who are able to share their faith with their grandchildren can use this book as a way to help teach them the basic Catholic prayers. Parents who choose to homeschool their children will find the prayer experiences in this book easy to use as they help their children develop a relationship with God.

No matter which prayer or practice you choose, may it deepen your relationship with God and fill the need your soul has as you journey into the heart of God.

# 1. SIGN OF THE CROSS

**Catechist background**

The practice of beginning prayers by tracing the sign of the cross is prominent in the Catholic Church. In the early days of the church, a small sign of the cross was traced on one's forehead using the thumb or finger.

Scripture provides us with the symbolism of the sign of the cross. The shape of the sign of the cross reminds us of the cross on which Jesus died. It also reminds us of the Trinity: Father, Son, and Holy Spirit.

The sign of the cross is used in the rites of the sacraments. In baptism, the sign of the cross is made on the forehead of the person being baptized to remind us that the cross is one of the main mysteries of our faith. The words of baptism—"I baptize you in the name of the Father, and of the Son, and of the Holy Spirit," taken from Matthew's gospel (Matthew 28:19)—are spoken while the water is poured or while the one to be baptized is immersed. This reminds us of the Triune God.

In the rite of the anointing of the sick, the priest anoints the sick person on the forehead; he makes the sign of the cross while praying: "Through this holy anointing may the Lord in his love and mercy help you with the grace of the Holy Spirit. Amen." He also anoints the sick person on the hands, making the sign of the cross while praying: "May the Lord who frees you from sin save you and raise you up. Amen."

When a bishop administers the sacrament of confirmation, he anoints each person to be confirmed. He makes the sign of the cross on the forehead while he prays: "Be sealed with the gift of the Holy Spirit."

During the sacrament of reconciliation, after the penitent has confessed his or her sins and made an act of contrition, the priest makes the sign of the cross while praying: "I absolve you from your sins in the name of the Father, and of the Son, and of the Holy Spirit."

Although this is a short prayer, the challenge in teaching it to others is getting the correct hand placement with the right words. (Hint: left shoulder before right shoulder because "l" comes before "r" in the alphabet.)

**Prayer**

*In the name of the Father, and of the Son, and of the Holy Spirit. Amen.*

### SIGN OF THE CROSS LESSON PLAN 1

**Objectives**
- ☐ To learn the sign of the cross with the words and gestures
- ☐ To learn the symbols of the sign of the cross found in Scripture

**Materials**
- ☐ **5 SPRING-TYPE WOODEN CLOTHESPINS**
- ☐ **PERMANENT BLACK MARKER**
- ☐ **UPPER-BODY SILHOUETTE TEMPLATE** *traced on cardboard and folded in half lengthwise so the crease may be used to place the second and fifth clothespins on the chest*

**Lesson**
- After you gather the children around you, discuss the sign of the cross and how we use it to begin our prayers, including the prayer of the Mass.
- Acquaint them with the biblical symbols of the sign of the cross: the cross Jesus died on and the three persons in the Trinity.
- Use the activity with the clothespins and torso template to practice the words and gestures of the sign of the cross.
- Make the sign of the cross together, stressing that it should be done slowly and reverently.
- If time permits take the children over to church

to the holy water fonts. Have each individual child make the sign of the cross after they dip their right hand into the holy water.

## Clothespin activity

❶ Print the following words on each clothespin with permanent marker:
- Clothespin One: In the name of the Father
- Clothespin Two: and of the Son
- Clothespin Three: and of the Holy
- Clothespin Four: Spirit
- Clothespin Five: Amen

❷ Using the upper-body silhouette *(page 8)*, children clip the clothespins to the part of the body where our hand goes as we make the sign of the cross. Two will be placed on the chest area.

### SIGN OF THE CROSS LESSON PLAN 2

### Objectives
☐ To be aware of the different sacraments that use the sign of the cross
☐ To be able to make the sign of the cross correctly

### Materials
☐ **CROSS TEMPLATE** *(The cross could be traced on the black paper prior to class)*
☐ **8.5" X 11" PIECES OF BLACK CONSTRUCTION PAPER**, *one per child*
☐ **TOOTHPICKS**
☐ **YARN**
☐ **MARKERS/CRAYONS**
☐ **SACRAMENT HANDOUT**, *one page per child*

### Lesson
- Gather the children and begin the lesson by using the background information to discuss each sacrament that uses the sign of the cross.
- Review the meaning of the sign of the cross prayer and ask children to give other examples of when this prayer is said.
- Let each child make the sign of the cross on another person's hands while praying "In the name of the Father, and of the Son, and of the Holy Spirit. Amen."
- Give directions on how to complete the sign of the cross sacrament activity.
- Let each child make the sign of the cross and pray their favorite prayer.

## Sign of the cross sacrament activity

❶ Give each student a large piece of construction paper with a cross traced on it. Or have the children trace the cross on the black paper using the template *(page 9)*.

❷ Fill in the cross template by gluing toothpicks. Some toothpicks may have to be cut to fit.

❸ Decorate the four sacrament templates.

❹ Punch four holes at the bottom of the black construction paper.

❺ Punch holes at the top of the sacrament templates.

❻ Use yarn to tie the sacrament templates to the black construction paper.

❼ Encourage the children to take their sacrament cross home and tell their family about how the sign of the cross is used in the sacraments.

# SIGN OF THE CROSS **LESSON PLAN 1**
*Clothespin activity*

## SIGN OF THE CROSS **LESSON PLAN 2**
*Sign of the cross sacrament activity*

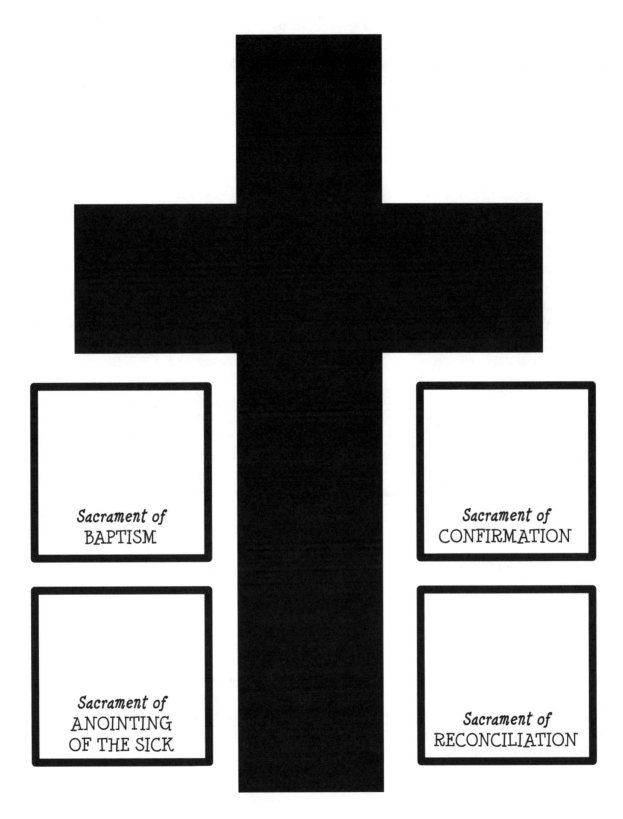

# 2  THE **OUR FATHER**
## (THE LORD'S PRAYER)

**Catechist background**

The Our Father is commonly referred to as the "Lord's Prayer," not because Jesus prayed it but because he taught it to the disciples. We pray this prayer at every Mass.

The Our Father is found in the Bible in two different places. Saint Luke (Luke 11:2–4) has one version of the prayer, and Saint Matthew (Matthew 6:9–13) has another. Perhaps this is because Jesus actually taught it more than once and, as the prayer was passed down orally, it was remembered somewhat differently. The recitation of the Our Father is part of the baptism ritual as well as part of the Liturgy of the Hours (the official daily prayer of the church). The Our Father is also included when we pray the rosary.

As you teach this basic prayer, have the students imagine that they are listening to Jesus teach them how to pray just as he did the disciples.

**Prayer**

*Our Father, who art in heaven, hallowed be your name; your kingdom come; your will be done on earth as it is in heaven. Give us this day our daily bread, and forgive us our trespasses, as we forgive those who trespass against us; and lead us not into temptation, but deliver us from evil. Amen.*

## OUR FATHER **LESSON PLAN 1**

**Objectives**
- ☐ To practice saying the Our Father by using a prayer ball (see phrases to write on the ball)
- ☐ To learn important words from the Our Father by solving a crossword puzzle

**Materials**
- ☐ **LARGE BEACH BALL OR RUBBER BALL**
- ☐ **CROSSWORD PUZZLE HANDOUT**

**Lesson**
- Gather the students and point out the words of the Our Father on the board or chart paper.
- Talk about what each phrase of the Our Father means.
- Read the Our Father together two or three times prayerfully.
- Use the prayer ball.
- Explain the crossword puzzle; then give time for students to complete it.
- Gather in your prayer space, and conclude the lesson by praying the Our Father together.

### Prayer ball activity

❶ Using a permanent marker, put a large dot on the ball and a phrase of the Our Father (see phrase list below). Continue placing dots and phrases until the entire prayer is on the ball. Gather the children in a large circle. Throw the ball back and forth. When the person catches the ball, he or she must begin reciting the Our Father, beginning with the phrase closest to the person's right thumb. If the student cannot continue saying the Our Father from the point where his or her thumb lands, allow the student to read it from the display.

Phrases for ball:
- Our Father, who art in heaven
- Hallowed be your name
- Your kingdom come
- Your will be done
- On earth as it is in heaven
- Give us this day
- Our daily bread
- And forgive us our trespasses
- As we forgive those who trespass against us
- And lead us not into temptation
- But deliver us from evil. Amen.

## Crossword puzzle activity

❶ Use the words from the Our Father to solve the crossword puzzle *(page 12)*.

---

### OUR FATHER **LESSON PLAN 2**

**Objectives**
- ☐ To learn the Our Father by playing the Amen card game
- ☐ To compare Matthew's version to Luke's version

**Materials**
- ☐ **AMEN CARDS** *(page 13), copied on heavy paper or cardstock*
- ☐ **DRAWING PAPER**
- ☐ **MARKERS/CRAYONS**

**Lesson**
- Gather the students and display the Our Father found in Matthew 6:9–13.
- Ask if it is similar to the one prayed at Mass or used in the rosary.
- Display the Our Father found in Luke 11:2–4.
- Talk about how it is similar to the one in Matthew, and discuss how it is different.
- Discuss which one the students like better and why.
- Ask students to draw a picture of Jesus teaching the disciples this prayer. Tell them to put themselves into the picture.
- Explain the Amen card game. Organize the students into small groups. Distribute one set of cards to each group and have them play the game.
- Conclude the lesson by praying the Our Father together.

## Amen card game activity
[2 or more players]

*Preparation:* Cut out two of every card except the Amen card. There should be only one Amen card.

*Goal:* To avoid being the player who ends the game holding the Amen card.

*Setup:* Choose a dealer. Deal the cards as evenly as possible among the players. It is acceptable for some players to have more cards than other players.

*Game play:* Players sort their cards and discard any pairs. The dealer then offers his hand, face down, to the player on his left. That player randomly takes one card from the dealer. If the card matches one he already has in his hand, he puts the pair down. If not, he keeps it. Play proceeds clockwise; so the player to the left of the dealer then offers his hand, face down, to the player on his left. This cycle repeats until there are no more pairs and the only remaining card is the Amen card.

*Winning:* The game ends when the Amen card is the only card in play. The persons not holding the Amen card are the winners.

# OUR FATHER **LESSON PLAN 1**
*Crossword puzzle activity*

**Word Bank**
GIVE
DAILY
HALLOWED
FORGIVE
TEMPTATION
DELIVER
BREAD
HEAVEN
FATHER
EARTH
NAME
EVIL
DAY
TRESPASS
AMEN
KINGDOM

**ACROSS**
2. To offer something to another person
3. A period of 24 hours
6. A person's identification
10. To show mercy
11. To do something every day
13. The planet we live on
15. The desire to do something wrong
16. To hand over

**DOWN**
1. Food made of flour, water, and yeast
4. Word said at the end of a prayer
5. The spiritual domain
7. Very bad
8. To enter someplace without permission
9. To honor as holy
12. Creator of heaven and earth
14. The home of God and the angels

## OUR FATHER **LESSON PLAN 2**
*Amen card game activity*

- Our Father,
- who art in heaven,
- hallowed be thy name;
- thy kingdom come, thy will be done
- on earth as it is in heaven.
- Give us this day our daily bread,
- and forgive us our trespasses,
- as we forgive those who trespass against us;
- and lead us not into temptation,
- but deliver us from evil.
- *Amen*

# 3 THE **GLORY BE** (DOXOLOGY)

**Catechist background**

The Glory Be prayer was created in order to help people understand and express the truths of the Catholic faith. It is comforting to know there is a short prayer that contains some very basic beliefs.

The phrase "Glory be to the Father, to the Son, and to the Holy Spirit" was first used around the year 300 to remind people that Jesus used these words when he taught the disciples to go out and baptize (Matthew 28:19). The prayer also focuses on the Blessed Trinity; there are three divine persons in one God. Each person in the Trinity has a specific role. God the Father is the creator as well as the one who chooses us and calls us to be sons and daughters. God the Son shows us God the Father, and redeems us by his death on the cross. God the Holy Spirit gives us new life and witnesses to God the Son.

The next section of the prayer—"As it was in the beginning, is now, and ever shall be, world without end"—came later. This phrase confirmed that there really are three persons in one God. The Glory Be prayer is said at the end of each decade of the rosary.

There are also longer versions of the Glory Be prayer. If you look carefully at the Gloria found in the Mass, it has the same basic faith beliefs.

**Prayer**

*Glory be to the Father, and to the Son, and to the Holy Spirit; as it was in the beginning, is now, and ever shall be, world without end. Amen.*

## GLORY BE **LESSON PLAN 1**

**Objectives**
- ☐ To learn the Glory Be prayer through making shamrock hats
- ☐ To sequence the Glory Be by putting phrases in order

**Materials**
- ☐ **PAPER** *for making a white band that will fit around each child's head*
- ☐ **GREEN CONSTRUCTION PAPER** *for making shamrocks*
- ☐ **SHAMROCK TEMPLATE** *(page 16)*
- ☐ **BLACK FINE POINT MARKERS**
- ☐ **PHRASES OF THE PRAYER HANDOUT** *run off on cardstock, two pages per child*

**Lesson**
- Gather the students together. Discuss the idea that the Glory Be is a very short prayer that contains some of our basic beliefs as Catholics. Talk about the mystery of the Trinity, three persons in one God: God the Father, God the Son, and God the Holy Spirit. Tell how shamrocks are symbols that are sometimes used to illustrate the Trinity.
- Explain that this prayer is used as we pray the rosary.
- Display the words of the Glory Be on the board or chart paper. Pray it with the children.
- Use the template to make a Glory Be hat.
- At the end of the class, send home the parent letter along with the shamrock hats and the materials for the game "Pop."

## Shamrock hat activity

❶ Use a strip of paper 2 ½ inches wide and long enough to fit around the child's head.
❷ Make four shamrocks. Write the words for the Glory Be as follows: shamrock one: Glory be to the Father; shamrock two: and to the Son, and to the Holy Spirit; shamrock three: as it was in the beginning, is now, and ever shall be; shamrock four: world without end. Amen.
❸ Glue the shamrocks on the band.

## "Pop" [A game for 2 or more players]

❶ Cut the phrases into strips *(page 17)*. Cut out the two "pop" strips too. Mix all the strips up in a large coffee can. Players take turns pulling the strips out of the can. The object of the game is to put the prayer in order. If someone draws a phrase that he or she already has, the player puts the strip back. If a player draws the "pop" strip, he or she must return all of his or her strips to the can and start over. The first player to complete the entire prayer wins.

### GLORY BE **LESSON PLAN 2**

### Objectives

☐ To become familiar with Bible stories focusing on the roles of the Trinity
☐ To learn two beliefs about each person in the Trinity by creating a Trinity mobile

### Materials
☐ **Bible**
☐ **Yarn**
☐ **Hole punch**
☐ **Construction paper** *for making triangles*
☐ **Triangle templates**

### Lesson

- Gather the students and display the words of the Glory Be prayer.
- Read Genesis 1:1–31 and Genesis 2:1–4 and discuss the role of God the Father as Creator.
- Read Mark 15:22–41 and discuss God the Son (Jesus), redeeming us out of love.
- Read Acts 2:1–4 and discuss the coming of the Holy Spirit on the first Pentecost.
- Direct the children to make a Trinity mobile.
- Pray the Glory Be prayer together.

### Trinity mobile activity

❶ Make a large triangle. Write the Glory Be prayer on it.
❷ Make three smaller triangles. On the first triangle, write "God the Father" and two beliefs about God as Father.
❸ On the second triangle, write "God the Son" and two beliefs about God as Son.
❹ On the third triangle, write "God the Holy Spirit" and two beliefs about God as Spirit.
❺ Use different lengths of yarn to attach the smaller triangles to the large triangle. Remind everyone of the Trinity by hanging the Trinity mobile in a room in your house.

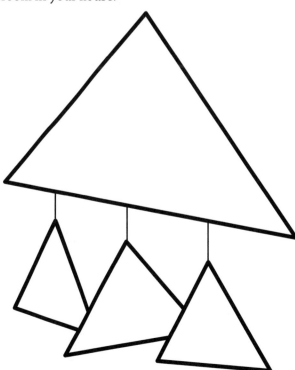

**GLORY BE LESSON PLAN 1**
*Shamrock hat activity*

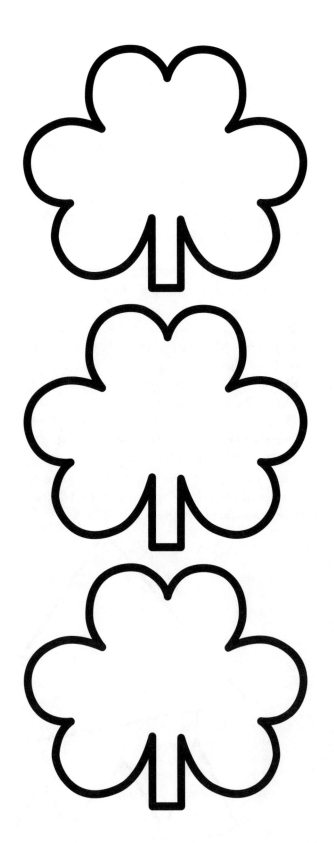

## Letter to parents

Dear Parents,
Today, our class focused on learning the Glory Be prayer that is prayed as part of the rosary. Your child is wearing a shamrock hat, which we made after praying this prayer together. We talked about the three persons in the Trinity: God the Father, God the Son, and God the Holy Spirit. Please practice this prayer at home with your child. Described below is a simple game that you can play with your child. It's easy to make, fun to play, and reinforces the prayer. I know your entire family will enjoy this game!

Sincerely,

Cut the phrases into strips *(page 17)*. Cut out the two "pop" strips too. Have one full set of strips for each person participating in the game. Mix all the strips up in a large coffee can. Players take turns pulling the strips out of the can. The object of the game is to put the prayer in order. If someone draws a phrase that he or she already has, the player puts the strip back. If a player draws the "pop" strip, he or she must return all of his or her strips to the can and start over. The first player to complete the entire prayer wins.

# GLORY BE **LESSON PLAN 1**
*"Pop" game activity*

| |
|---|
| **« Pop »** |
| **« Pop »** |
| **Glory be** |
| **to the Father** |
| **and to the Son** |
| **and to the Holy Spirit** |
| **as it was** |
| **in the beginning** |
| **is now** |
| **and ever shall be** |
| **world without end** |
| **Amen.** |

# 4 THE HAIL MARY

## Catechist background

The Hail Mary is a prayer that Catholics recite often. It is the main prayer of the rosary. It is also said when a person prays the Angelus. The Hail Mary contains three of the five forms of prayer: praise, thanksgiving, and petition.

This prayer did not exist until the eleventh century. The monks at that time prayed very long offices (the official daily prayer of the church) each day. If the day celebrated a feast of the Blessed Mother, the monks also prayed the "Little Office" of Mary. The Little Office of Mary contained the words of the Archangel Gabriel to Mary, as well as the words of Elizabeth to Mary. The prayer was as follows: "Hail Mary, full of grace, the Lord is with thee; blessed art thou amongst women and blessed is the fruit of thy womb."

As time went on, not only did the monks pray this prayer, but the laity did too because they heard the monks praying it over and over again. In 1196, the Bishop of Paris asked his priests to begin teaching this prayer to everyone. Soon it was well known in the parishes. This is section one of the Hail Mary we currently use. Eventually, Pope Urban IV added the name of Jesus. Then, during the 1500s, it was decided that this beautiful prayer would be more complete if we asked Mary to pray for us; the last section was added at this time.

Each line of the Hail Mary is closely connected to two events in Scripture: the Annunciation and the Visitation.

| PRAYER | BIBLE VERSE |
|---|---|
| Hail Mary, full of grace | Luke 1:28 |
| the Lord is with you | Luke 1:28 |
| blessed are you among women | Luke 1:42 |
| blessed is the fruit of your womb, Jesus | Luke 1:42 |
| Holy Mary, Mother of God | Luke 1:43 |
| Pray for us sinners, now and at the hour of our death | James 5:16 |

## Prayer

*Hail Mary, full of grace, the Lord is with you; blessed are you among women, and blessed is the fruit of your womb, Jesus. Holy Mary, Mother of God, pray for us sinners, now and at the hour of our death. Amen.*

### HAIL MARY LESSON PLAN 1

## Objectives
☐ The children will learn the Hail Mary through song
☐ The children will learn the Hail Mary and what the prayer means through a word search

## Materials
☐ **COPIES OF THE WORD SEARCH** (page 20)

## Song
**Hail Mary** (Tune: Are You Sleeping?)

VERSE I
Hail Mary
Hail Mary
Full of Grace
Full of Grace
The Lord is with you
The Lord is with you
Blessed are you
Blessed are you

VERSE II
Among women
Among women
Blessed is the fruit
Blessed is the fruit
Of your womb, Jesus
Of your womb, Jesus
Holy Mary
Holy Mary

Verse III
Mother of God
Mother of God
Pray for us
Pray for us
Now and at the hour
Now and at the hour
Of our death
Of our death

**Lesson**
- Gather the children and discuss what they already know about Mary.
- Tell them the story of when Mary went to visit her cousin Elizabeth (Luke 1:39–56). Ask them how they would feel if Mary came to their home. What would they do?
- Teach the students the Hail Mary, using the song.
- Hand out the word search activity page for the children to complete.
- End the lesson by singing or praying the Hail Mary together.

### HAIL MARY **LESSON PLAN 2**

**Objectives**
- ☐ The children will learn about the Annunciation and the Visitation
- ☐ The children will make a prayer pennant

**Materials**
- ☐ **Prayer pennant templates** *(page 21)*
- ☐ **A Bible or children's Bible**

**Lesson**
- Gather the children and read them the stories of the Annunciation (Luke 1:26–38) and the Visitation (Luke 1:39–56).
- Compare the stories and discuss which story is their favorite, and why.
- (Optional: Read *The Lady of Guadalupe* by Tomie dePaola; and Saint Bernadette Soubirous and *Our Lady of Lourdes* by Anne Eileen Heffernan, FSP and Mary Elizabeth Tebo, FSP)
- Direct the children to make a prayer pennant in honor of Mary.

### Prayer pennant activity

❶ Have the children create a prayer pennant for one of the stories. Have them write their own prayer to Mary in the center of the pennant. The children can decorate their pennants with symbols and pictures. Invite the children to take their pennants home and hang them in a prominent place to remind others of Mary.

HAIL MARY **LESSON PLAN 1**
*Word search activity*

# Hail Mary

Find the following words in the word search. There will be eight letters that are not circled. Unscramble the eight letters to find the mystery words. Words can be found horizontally, vertically, diagonally, backwards and forwards.

AMONG
FRUIT
LORD
SINNERS
BLEST
GRACE
MOTHER
WOMB
DEATH
JESUS
PRAY
WOMEN

| E | P | R | A | Y | M | S | H |
|---|---|---|---|---|---|---|---|
| C | H | L | M | O | U | A | N |
| A | T | R | T | S | B | E | D |
| R | A | H | E | B | M | F | R |
| G | E | J | L | O | O | R | O |
| R | D | E | W | I | W | U | L |
| Y | S | R | E | N | N | I | S |
| T | A | M | O | N | G | T | A |

Mystery words:

\_ \_ \_ \_

\_ \_ \_ \_

20

# HAIL MARY **LESSON PLAN 2**
*Prayer pennant activity*

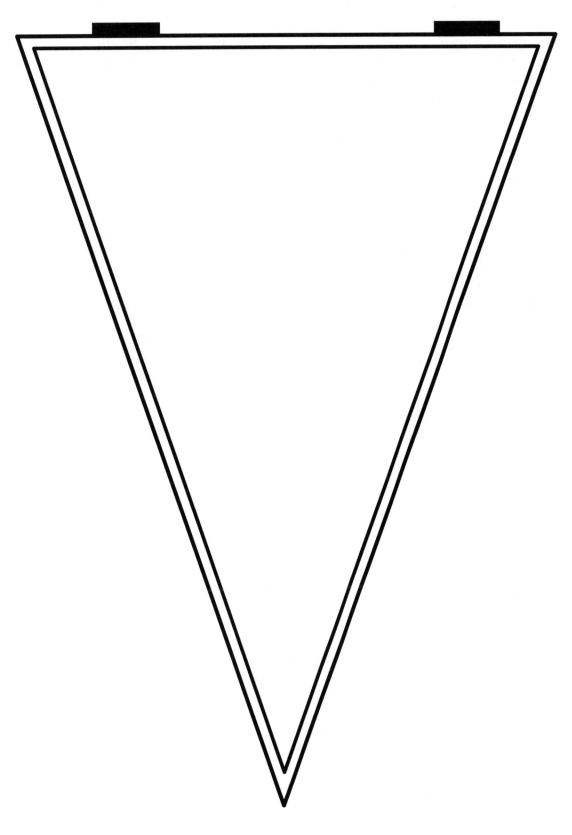

# 5 GUARDIAN ANGEL PRAYER

**Catechist background**

God gave each of us a guardian angel at our birth to watch over us, to pray for us, and to guide us. Angels can protect us from spiritual and physical harm. Jesus referred to angels when he said that children's "angels in heaven always see the face of my Father who is in heaven" (Matthew 18:10).

Many theologians and saints have referred to angels. St. Basil wrote "every one of the faithful has an angel at his side as educator and guide, directing his life." St. Clement and St. Gregory the Great believed that countries, cities, towns, and families had angels watching over them.

The word "angel" comes from the Greek work "angelos," which means "messenger." Angels are God's special messengers. Angels are found throughout the Scriptures. Raphael, an archangel, was sent to Tobit to heal his blindness (Tobit, chapter 11). Angels protected the three young men who were thrown in a fiery furnace by King Nebuchadnezzar (Daniel, chapter 3). Gabriel asked Mary to be the mother of Jesus (Luke 1:26–38). And remember when St. Peter was in prison? An angel rescued him (Acts 12:6–10).

*Archangels*

The biblical reference for the Archangel Raphael is found in the Book of Tobit. He was disguised as a man and journeyed with Tobit's son. After the journey, he healed Tobit of his blindness. The name Raphael means "God heals." He is the patron of the blind, of nurses and physicians, and of travelers.

The Archangel Michael is known for fighting the bad angels. Michael is mentioned in the Book of Daniel and in the Book of Revelation. The name Michael means "Who is like God." He is the patron of paratroopers, police, mariners, and grocers.

In the Bible, the Archangel Gabriel is found in the Book of Daniel and the Gospel of Luke. Catholics are most familiar with his role as the one who asked Mary to be the mother of God. Gabriel means "God is my strength." He is the patron of messengers, those who work for radio and television, and postal workers.

These three archangels are the only ones found in the Scriptures. Each one has a different job: Michael protects, Gabriel announces, and Raphael guides.

**Prayer**

*Angel of God, my guardian dear, to whom God's love commits me here, ever this day be at my side, to light and guard, to rule and guide. Amen.*

## GUARDIAN ANGEL PRAYER **LESSON PLAN 1**

**Objectives**
- ☐ Children will use song to discuss angels and what they do
- ☐ Children will recite the Guardian Angel prayer

**Materials**
- ☐ **ANGEL TEMPLATE** (run off on cardstock, if possible) (page 24)
- ☐ **HOLE PUNCH** (for younger children; or to save time, punch the holes in the templates prior to class)
- ☐ **YARN**

**Song**
**Angels** (Tune: Twinkle, Twinkle Little Star)

Angels, angels up in heaven
How I wonder what you do.
Guarding, guiding us today,
Keeps you busy all day long.
Angels, angels up in heaven
How I wonder what you do.

### Lesson

- Gather the children together and ask what they know about angels.
- Use the background material to talk about guardian angels and their main jobs.
- Give examples of how angels "light" our way, how they "guard" us, how they "guide" us.
- Ask students to share how they think their angels take care of them.
- Teach the "Angels" song.
- Explain the angel activity using the angel template and yarn.
- Pray together the Guardian Angel prayer to complete the lesson.

### GUARDIAN ANGEL PRAYER LESSON PLAN 2

#### Objectives

☐ To read and discuss the following biblical references to angels:
- *Tobit 5:1–17; 6:7–9; 11:7–14*
- *Revelation 12:7–9*
- *Luke 1:26–38*

☐ To make clouds to help the children remember what the archangels' names mean and what their main job is

#### Materials

☐ **White or blue construction paper**
☐ **Cloud template**
☐ **Scissors**
☐ **Markers**
☐ **Facial tissue**
☐ **Glue**

### Lesson

- Gather the children and read or tell the story from the Book of Tobit.
- Ask the children what their favorite part is and why. Ask if they would like to have a disguised angel go with them. Where would they like to go with the angel?
- Use the background information to talk about each archangel, what their main job is, and what their name means.
- Proceed to the angel clouds activity.
- To conclude the lesson, say the Guardian Angel prayer together.

### Angel clouds activity

1. Cut out six large clouds.
2. On cloud one, write the following: Archangel Raphael, whose name means "God has healed," healed Tobit from his blindness.
3. On cloud two, write the following: Archangel Gabriel, whose name means "God is my strength," asked Mary to be the mother of God.
4. On cloud three, write the following: Archangel Michael, whose name means "Who is like God," led the good angels in battle against the bad angels.
5. Glue the edges of cloud one to a blank cloud; leave a bit of space, and stuff the cloud with facial tissue to make it puffy. Finish gluing the edges of the cloud together. Do the same for the other two clouds. Glue the clouds in an arrangement so all three are connected with the words visible.

# GUARDIAN ANGEL PRAYER **LESSON PLAN 1**
## *Guardian angel activity*

Using yarn, go from hole to hole in the correct sequence to complete the Guardian Angel prayer. Take your angel template home and place it in your bedroom where your guardian angel can watch over you. Talk to your angel every day and thank the angel for taking care of you. Also, tell your guardian angel what you need to help you be a better person.

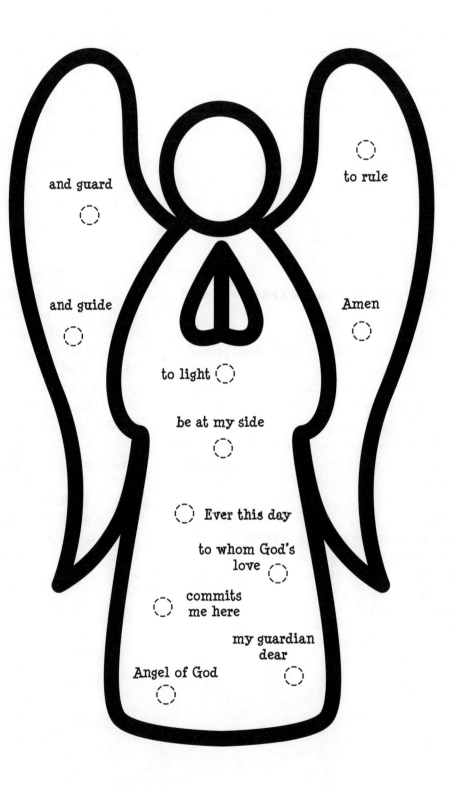

Labels on the angel template (with holes):
- and guard
- to rule
- and guide
- Amen
- to light
- be at my side
- Ever this day
- to whom God's love
- commits me here
- my guardian dear
- Angel of God

# GUARDIAN ANGEL PRAYER **LESSON PLAN 2**
## *Angel clouds activity*

## 6 APOSTLES' CREED

### Catechist background
The word "creed" comes from the Latin word "credo," meaning "I believe." A creed contains basic truths of the Catholic faith and fundamental beliefs about each person in the Trinity and the "job" each one has. The creed also reminds us of the timeline of salvation history.

The Apostles' Creed is the oldest creed we have. It is the foundation for the other creeds. This creed is rooted in apostolic times and reflects the beliefs of the apostles and their followers. As the early Christians were baptized, they professed their faith with the simple statement "I believe that Jesus is the Son of God," which was a very short creed. By the third century, a person to be baptized responded to three questions based on the Trinity.

Today's baptismal rite for children includes three questions that either the person to be baptized answers or the parents and godparents answer if the person being baptized is an infant. These three questions are 1) Do you believe in God, the Father almighty, creator of Heaven and earth? 2) Do you believe in Jesus Christ, his only Son, our Lord, who was born of the Virgin Mary, was crucified, died and was buried, rose from the dead, and is now seated at the right hand of the Father? 3) Do you believe in the Holy Spirit, the holy catholic Church, the communion of saints, the forgiveness of sins, the resurrection of the body, and life everlasting?

The statement "descended into hell" in the Apostles' Creed refers to Sheol or the place of the dead. Jesus visited those who died before he lived. It is not the place occupied by Satan and the bad angels.

In the past, the Apostles' Creed was used for liturgies with children because it was simpler and easier for them to understand; the new Roman Missal allows this creed to be used in all liturgies and commends its use especially during Lent and Easter. This creed reminds us of our baptismal promises, which we renew at Easter. The creed is also used at the beginning of the rosary.

### Prayer
*I believe in God, the Father almighty, Creator of heaven and earth, and in Jesus Christ, his only Son, our Lord, who was conceived by the Holy Spirit, born of the Virgin Mary, suffered under Pontius Pilate, was crucified, died and was buried; he descended into hell; on the third day he rose again from the dead; he ascended into heaven, and is seated at the right hand of God the Father almighty; from there he will come to judge the living and the dead. I believe in the Holy Spirit, the holy catholic Church, the communion of saints, the forgiveness of sins, the resurrection of the body, and life everlasting. Amen.*

### APOSTLES' CREED LESSON PLAN 1

### Objectives
☐ To know the meaning of the phrases about God the Father and God the Son
☐ To write a favorite phrase using Morse Code

### Materials
☐ **TEMPLATE OF THE MORSE CODE**
☐ **COPY OF THE APOSTLES' CREED**
☐ **MINI MARSHMALLOWS**
☐ **PRETZEL STICKS**

### Lesson
- Gather the children around you.
- Discuss the fact that the Apostles' Creed talks about God the Father, God the Son, and God the Holy Spirit.
- Talk about what the children know about God the Father, and relate it to the phrases in the creed.
- Talk about what the children know about God the Son, and relate it to the phrases in the creed.
- Direct the children to do the Morse Code activity *(page 28)*.

- Invite children to share which phrase they chose to do.

### APOSTLES' CREED **LESSON PLAN 2**

### Objectives
☐ To pray the Apostles' Creed beginning with any phrase
☐ To discuss the meaning of the Apostles' Creed beginning with God the Holy Spirit

### Materials
☐ **1 egg carton per student**
☐ **1 set of twelve Apostles' Creed strips per student** *(page 29)*
☐ **1 button per student**

### Lesson
- Gather the students around you.
- Discuss the meaning of each of the phrases beginning with God the Holy Spirit.
- Have the students prepare the egg carton.
- Play the Carton Creed activity.
- Practice praying the prayer together.

## Carton creed activity

**❶** Get an egg carton and paste each of the phrases in an "egg" section. Place a button in the egg carton. Close the lid of the egg carton and shake it. Open the lid. Can you recite the prayer beginning with the phrase where the button landed?

# APOSTLES' CREED **LESSON PLAN 1**
## *The Creed in Morse Code activity*

Sometimes, Christians had to use a code to communicate with each other so they wouldn't be arrested for believing in Jesus. Here is a copy of the Morse Code. Choose your favorite phrase from the Apostles' Creed; use marshmallows to represent the dots, and pretzel sticks to represent the dashes. Make your favorite phrase. Give it to a friend and see if he or she can figure it out.

## International Morse Code

| | | | | | |
|---|---|---|---|---|---|
| A | •— | N | —• | 1 | •———— |
| B | —••• | O | ——— | 2 | ••——— |
| C | —•—• | P | •——• | 3 | •••—— |
| D | —•• | Q | ——•— | 4 | ••••— |
| E | • | R | •—• | 5 | ••••• |
| F | ••—• | S | ••• | 6 | —•••• |
| G | ——• | T | — | 7 | ——••• |
| H | •••• | U | ••— | 8 | ———•• |
| I | •• | V | •••— | 9 | ————• |
| J | •——— | W | •—— | 0 | ————— |
| K | —•— | X | —••— | | |
| L | •—•• | Y | —•—— | | |
| M | —— | Z | ——•• | | |

A dash is equal to three dots

The space between parts of the same letter is equal to one dot

The space between two letters is equal to three dots (one dash)

The space between two words is equal to seven dots

**EXAMPLE**

God = ——•   ———   —••

## APOSTLES' CREED PRAYER **LESSON PLAN 2**
*Carton creed activity*

---

I believe in God, the Father almighty, Creator of heaven and earth

---

and in Jesus Christ, his only Son, our Lord,

---

who was conceived by the Holy Spirit

---

born of the Virgin Mary, suffered under Pontius Pilate

---

was crucified, died and was buried; he descended into hell;

---

on the third day he rose again from the dead;

---

he ascended into heaven

---

and is seated at the right hand of God the Father almighty;

---

from there he will come to judge the living and the dead.

---

I believe in the Holy Spirit, the holy catholic Church,

---

the communion of saints, the forgiveness of sins,

---

the resurrection of the body, and life everlasting. Amen.

*traditional prayers*

#  ACT OF CONTRITION

## Catechist background

An act of contrition is a simple, humble prayer of apology. There are three components necessary to all prayers of contrition. First, the person needs to acknowledge the infraction or how he or she has hurt another; next, the person shows remorse; finally, the person makes the intention to try not to do the same action again. An act of contrition is prayed so an individual can express sorrow for sin and repair the relationship with God.

An act of contrition is prayed whenever a person receives the sacrament of reconciliation. The priest will ask that person to make an act of contrition after acknowledging his or her sins. The act of contrition may be a formal one (memorized) or the person may make up a spontaneous one as long as it contains the three previously discussed components. A person may also pray this prayer before going to bed each night in order to ask God's forgiveness for anything that might have hurt the relationship with God throughout the day.

Honesty is one of the virtues to focus on with students. In Proverbs 12:22 we read "Lying lips are an abomination to the Lord, but those who act faithfully are his delight." Another Scripture reference is 2 Corinthians 8:21, where we find "For we intend to do what is right not only in the Lord's sight but also in the sight of others." In Colossians 3:9 we find "Do not lie to one another, seeing that you have put off the old self with its practices." All three of these quotes encourage students to be honest at all times.

(Optional: There are several wonderful children's books that focus on honesty; any of these are great discussion starters. My favorites are 1) *The Empty Pot* by Demi, 2) *The Honest-to-Goodness Truth* by Patricia McKissack, 3) *Liar, Liar, Pants on Fire* by Diane deGroat, and 4) *Ruthie and the (Not So) Teeny Tiny Lie* by Laura Rankin.)

## Prayer

*My God, I am sorry for my sins with all my heart. In choosing to do wrong and failing to do good, I have sinned against you whom I should love above all things. I firmly intend, with your help, to do penance, to sin no more, and to avoid whatever leads me to sin. Our Savior Jesus Christ suffered and died for us. In his name, my God, have mercy. Amen.*

## ACT OF CONTRITION **LESSON PLAN**

### Objectives
☐ To discuss times we need to apologize
☐ To know the components necessary in an apology
☐ To learn the act of contrition

### Materials
☐ **CIRCLE TEMPLATE** *(page 31)*
☐ **CONSTRUCTION PAPER**
☐ **GLUE**
☐ **SCISSORS**

### Lesson
- Gather the students around you.
- Talk about times we need to apologize.
- How does it feel to make an apology? How does it feel to receive an apology?
- Using the background information, discuss the three components necessary for an apology.
- Give directions to role-play making apologies, using examples from students' daily lives.
- Introduce the act of contrition, and direct the children to make contrition caterpillars.
- To conclude the lesson, pray the act of contrition together.

# ACT OF CONTRITION **LESSON PLAN**
## *Contrition caterpillar activity*

Cut out the caterpillar sections. Color them and paste them in the correct order on a piece of construction paper. Take your caterpillar home and put it in your bedroom. Pray the act of contrition each night with your family.

- I firmly intend, with your help,
- (caterpillar head)
- In choosing to do wrong and failing to do good,
- to do penance, to sin no more,
- In his name, my God, have mercy. Amen
- Our Savior Jesus Christ suffered and died for us.
- and to avoid whatever leads me to sin.
- I have sinned against you whom I should love above all things.
- My God, I am sorry for my sins with all my heart.

# 8 MEAL PRAYER

## Catechist background
Catholics pray before meals, giving thanks to God for the food we are going to eat. At times we pray a short prayer, and at other times we pray a longer prayer, giving thanks for the many gifts God gives us throughout the day. No matter whether the prayer is long or short, we are following in the footsteps of Jesus, who prayed before meals.

When Jesus multiplied the loaves and fishes and fed well over 5000 people, he began this miracle by "giving thanks" (Matthew 14:19–21). At the Last Supper, before Jesus passed the cup and the bread to his disciples and told them to eat and drink his body and blood, he gave thanks. In chapter 24 of Luke's gospel, we find Jesus walking with the disciples on the road to Emmaus. When he stopped to eat with them, he "took bread, gave thanks, broke it, and gave it to them."

When we give thanks to God for providing for us, we recognize that everything we have comes from God (Romans 11:36). Praying before we eat reminds us of the many ways God blesses us throughout our lives.

## Prayer
*Bless us, O Lord, and these thy gifts, which we are about to receive through Christ our Lord. Amen.*

## MEAL PRAYER LESSON PLAN 1

### Objectives
- ☐ To know the order of the words found in the meal prayer
- ☐ To know the meals in which Jesus gave thanks

### Materials
- ☐ **9 PAPER SPOONS FOR EACH CHILD**, *run off on colored paper (page 34)*
- ☐ **9 PAPER SPOONS FOR EACH CHILD**, *run off on white paper (page 34)*
- ☐ **PENCILS**

### Lesson
- Gather the students around you and talk about the prayer before meals.
- Read the story of the loaves and fishes in Matthew 14:19–21, and discuss how Jesus gave thanks.
- Read the story of the Last Supper in Matthew 26:26–28, and discuss how it is similar to the story of the loaves and fishes.
- Read the story of the disciples on the road to Emmaus in Luke 24:28–32, and discuss how these three stories—the loaves and fishes, the Last Supper, and Jesus on the road to Emmaus—show us how to give thanks before we eat.
- Have students draw one of these scenes and then print the word "Thanks" at the bottom of the picture.
- Explain the Spoons of Thankfulness activity.
- If time allows, end class with the meal prayer and enjoy a simple snack.

# traditional prayers

## Spoons of thankfulness activity

❶ Give every student 9 spoons run off in one color. On each spoon print one of the following words: Bless, O, And, Thy, We, About, Receive, Christ, Lord.

❷ Give each student 9 spoons run off on white paper. On each spoon print one of the following words: Us, Lord, These, Gifts, Are, To, Through, Our, Amen.

❸ Put all of the spoons turned word-side down on a flat surface. Draw out one spoon from the colored paper and one from white paper. If the colored paper word follows the white spoon word, place the spoon on top of the white spoon. If the colored spoon word does not follow the white spoon, return both spoons. Whoever has the most pairs wins.

## MEAL PRAYER LESSON PLAN 2

### Objectives
☐ To remind students to pray before every meal
☐ To discuss healthy eating
☐ To see everything we have as a gift from God
☐ To share the story of St. Paul praying before meals in Acts 27:27–35

### Materials
☐ **12" Paper plates**, *one for each child*
☐ **Markers/Crayons**
☐ **Magazines with pictures of food**
☐ **11.5" x 17" construction paper**, *one sheet per child*
☐ **Glue**

### Lesson
- Gather the children around you.
- Read or tell the story of St. Paul in Acts 27:27–35.
- Discuss the concept that everything we have is a gift from God.
- Talk about healthy eating practices. Have students brainstorm healthy food choices. (Note: For more information on healthy eating practices see "My Plate" at www.choosemyplate.gov and use the foods listed in each section.)
- Discuss their favorite meals.
- Direct the children to complete the My Plate activity.
- Pray spontaneous "Thank you, God, for…" prayers.

## My plate activity

❶ Get a paper plate.
❷ Divide it into the four "My Plate" sections.
❸ Either draw or find pictures of your favorite foods and put them in the correct "My Plate" section.
❹ Color the Meal Prayer words (*page 35*).
❺ Glue the plate on a piece of construction paper.
❻ Glue the Meal Prayer words under the "plate" on the construction paper.

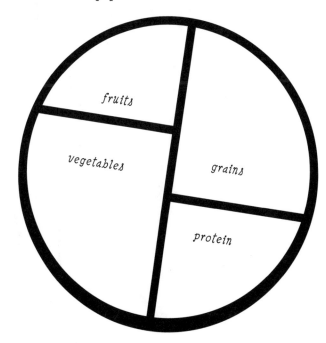

# MEAL PRAYER **LESSON PLAN 1**
*Spoons of thankfulness activity*

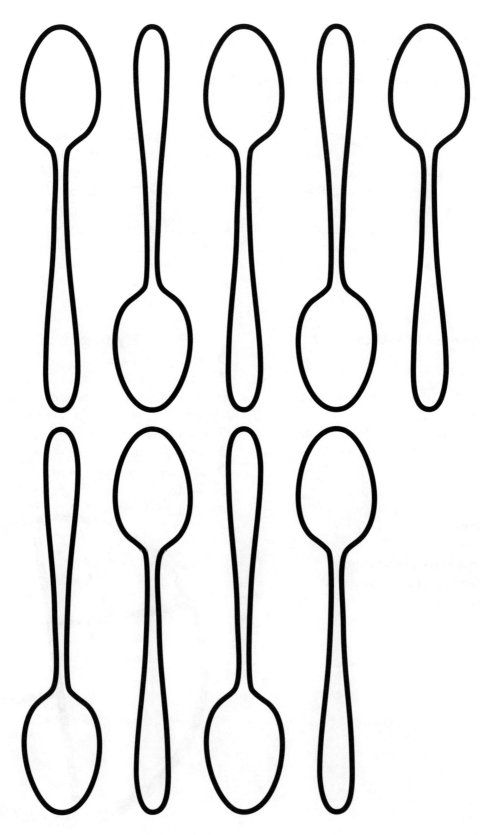

# MEAL PRAYER **LESSON PLAN 2**
*My plate activity*

# Bless us O Lord and these thy gifts which we are about to receive through Christ our Lord Amen

forms of prayer

 # INTERCESSION

## Catechist background

All of our prayers can be sorted into several, often closely related, categories: contrition, gratitude, intercession, blessing, and praise. Let's look at the prayers of intercession, which are also at times referred to as prayers of petition. In these prayers, we focus on asking God for things we need or for things others need. These prayers are simple and direct. Many people pray these prayers throughout their day. "God, please heal my spouse." Or "God, please help me on this test." During the Mass, the general intercessions, which are examples of petition, occur after the Creed. If you closely examine the Our Father, you will see that it consists of seven petitions. By teaching his disciples the Our Father, Jesus showed us how important our petitions are to God.

### INTERCESSION LESSON PLAN

## Objectives
☐ To learn the five forms of prayer by singing a song
☐ To write prayers of intercession

## Materials
☐ **Song copies** (page 37)
☐ **Small flower pots**
☐ **Flower template** (page 37)
☐ **Markers**
☐ **Construction paper**
☐ **Popsicle sticks**

## Lesson
- Gather the children around you.
- Discuss the names of the types of prayers.
- Focus on the prayer of petition. Discuss needs that people may have, and tell children they may pray for others and what they need. They may also ask God for things they need. Allow children to offer prayers of petition.
- Teach the Prayer Song.

## Prayer pots activity

*(This activity continues for the next several lessons)*

❶ Get a small flower pot.
❷ Put Styrofoam in it.
❸ Cut out five yellow flower centers. On one center write "Praise," on another "Sorrow," on another "Ask," on another "Bless," and on the last one "Thanks."
❹ Cut out eight petals for each flower.
❺ Write a petition prayer on some of the petals.
❻ Glue the petals onto the center.
❼ Glue the flower blossom onto a popsicle stick.
❽ Put the popsicle stick in the flower pot.
❾ Save the other centers and petals for the next lessons.

# INTERCESSION **LESSON PLAN**
## *Prayer pots activity*

### SONG
# Prayer Song
(Tune: Row, Row Your Boat)

**VERSE 1**

Pray, pray, pray to God

Pray with all your heart

Asking, thanking, praising, sorrow

God listens to them all

**VERSE 2**

Ask, ask, ask of God

What you need the most

Healing, blessing, trusting, hoping

God gives us all we need

**VERSE 3**

Thank, thank, thank our God

For his wondrous gifts

Daily bread and daily love

Remind us of God's grace

**VERSE 4**

Praise, praise, praise our God

Tell him how he's great

Creating, sharing, caring, loving

Awesome is our God

**VERSE 5**

Tears, tears, tears of sorrow

For not loving God

Hurting, ignoring, disbelieving

He'll always take us back

**VERSE 6**

Bless, bless, bless with hands

Open to give

Helping, holding, squeezing, clapping

God blesses us forever

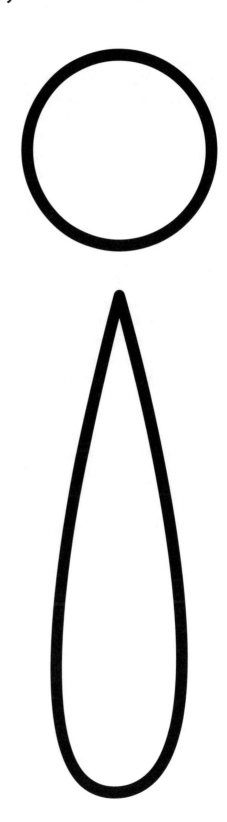

forms of prayer

## 10 PETITION

### Catechist background

The Our Father consists of seven petitions. The first petition is "Hallowed be thy name." Here, we are asking God to continue to call us to holiness because we know that God is holy. The next petition, "Thy kingdom come," refers to the end of the world. We are aware that our present faith life connects directly to experiencing the fullness of God's presence at the end of the world. The third petition, "Thy will be done on earth as it is heaven," encourages us to pray so we may know what God calls us to do and have the strength to do it. "Give us this day our daily bread" is the next petition. We trust God to take care of our needs. We also depend on each other; for each of us is the hands and the feet of God. The next petition, "Forgive us our trespasses as we forgive those who trespass against us," is one of the most challenging. In order to receive the mercy of God, we must offer mercy to each other. The sixth petition is "Lead us not into temptation"; we know we are easily led to sin. Our eyes and our hearts easily wander away from being focused on God. The final petition is "But deliver us from evil"; we know God can protect us from evil, and we know we need God's help. In conclusion, the first three petitions focus on God's glory, and the last four petitions focus on what we want God to give us.

### PETITION **LESSON PLAN**

**Objectives**
- ☐ To recognize that the Our Father consists of seven petitions
- ☐ To match the Our Father petition to its definition

**Materials**
- ☐ **LOLLIPOP CIRCLE**
- ☐ **LOLLIPOP STICK TEMPLATE**
- ☐ **HEAVY CARDBOARD**

**Lesson**
- Gather the children around you.
- Using the information above, begin discussing the phrases of the Our Father and what they mean.
- Be sure to emphasize that all of these phrases are petitions.
- Ask children if they can think of any other phrases in traditional prayers that are petitions.

### Petition pops activity

❶ Each student should color each of the pops and each of the "sticks."
❷ Glue them on heavy cardboard. Cut them out.
❸ Match each stick to the correct pop. Glue the stick onto the pop. For example, Pop One should have the stick "continue to call us to be holy."

*Pop One: Hallowed be your name*
*Pop Two: Thy kingdom come*
*Pop Three: Thy will be done on earth as it is in heaven*
*Pop Four: Give us this day our daily bread*
*Pop Five: Forgive us our trespasses as we forgive those who trespass against us*
*Pop Six: Lead us not into temptation*
*Pop Seven: But deliver us from evil*

# PETITION **LESSON PLAN**
## *Petition pops activity*

- Continue to call us to be holy.
- The end of the world will come some day.
- Listening to God will help us know what God wants us to do.
- God will take care of our needs.
- We must forgive each other just as God forgives us.
- Help us stay away from sin.
- Protect us from the devil.

- Thy kingdom come
- Hallowed be your name
- Thy will be done on earth as it is in heaven
- Give us this day our daily bread
- Forgive us our trespasses as we forgive those who trespass against us
- Lead us not into temptation
- But deliver us from evil

# 11 CONTRITION

### Catechist background

As we prepare to enter God's presence in prayer, we often prepare ourselves by petitioning God for forgiveness. At some time in our lives, all of us have those moments when we hurt others. It's important to apologize to the person we've hurt as well as let God know we are also sorry. According to the *Catechism of the Catholic Church*, this prayer type is called petition although many of us learned it as contrition. The best part of this prayer is that God is already waiting for us and loves us when we are our best self as well as when we are our worst self. For most of us, this is a very difficult prayer because when we are disappointed in ourselves, it can be difficult to believe deep down that God still loves us. We have experienced so much conditional love in our life that the experiences of unconditional love are almost unfathomable.

## CONTRITION LESSON PLAN 1

### Objectives
☐ To be aware of times when we hurt God or others
☐ To acknowledge that we are sorry when we hurt others

### Materials
☐ **LARGE CONSTRUCTION PAPER** *(Variety of Colors)*
☐ **MARKERS**
☐ **HEART TEMPLATE**

### Lesson
- Gather the children around you.
- Discuss the names of the types of prayers.
- Focus on the prayer of petition. Ask the children if they have ever hurt someone? Has someone hurt them? What feelings did they have? What did they say to the person they hurt? How does it feel when we tell someone we're sorry?
- From the previous lesson, get the flower center that says "Petition."
- Get the eight previously cut out petals.
- Write an "I'm sorry" prayer on each petal.
- Glue the petals onto the center.
- Glue the flower blossom onto a popsicle stick.
- Put the popsicle stick in the flower pot.
- Sing the Prayer Song.

### Trees of sorrow activity

1. Get a large sheet of construction paper.
2. Lay your forearm and hand on the construction paper beginning at the bottom.
3. Spread out your fingers.
4. Trace your forearm and fingers; however, do not trace the tip of your fingers. Leave it open.
5. Your forearm is the tree trunk and your fingers are the branches.
6. Write the words "I'm sorry" on the tree trunk.
7. Trace eight or nine hearts *(page 42)*. On some of the hearts write things that you're sorry you did. For example: I'm sorry I didn't share my toys with my friend.
8. Glue the hearts around the tree.
9. Hang your tree in the kitchen.

## CONTRITION LESSON PLAN 2

### Catechist background
The prayer before receiving Communion at Mass is a penitential prayer. Catholics realize that we are sinners and we do not receive Jesus in a state of perfection. Each day, we try not to sin and to come to Jesus with humility and love. This prayer is based on the words spoken by the centurion in Matthew's gospel. The centurion said, "Lord, I am not worthy to receive you, but only say the word and my servant shall be healed" (Matthew 8:8). Jesus wants to be with us in the Eucharist. He once told St. Faustina: "when I come to a human

# forms of prayer

heart in Holy Communion, my hands are full of all sorts of graces which I want to give to the soul."

**Objectives**
☐ To review prayers of petition
☐ To discuss the prayer before receiving Eucharist
☐ To make a bumper sticker using words from the prayer before receiving Eucharist

**Materials**
☐ **Prayer:**
> Lord, I am not worthy
> that you should enter under my roof,
> but only say the word
> and my soul shall be healed.

☐ **Bumper Sticker Template**
☐ **Markers**

**Lesson**
- Gather the students around you.
- Read the story in Matthew and discuss what the centurion meant.
- Review what it means to receive Jesus in the Eucharist.
- Review the type of attitude we need to have when we receive Jesus.
- Discuss each phrase of the prayer.
- Ask the students if they have heard this prayer before. If so, where?
- Ask students to listen for this prayer the next time they attend Mass.
- Pray the prayer together.

## Prayer before communion bumper sticker activity

❶ Give each child a bumper sticker template *(page 43)*. Ask each child to choose his or her favorite phrase from the prayer that was discussed. Have the child print the phrase on the bumper sticker template and decorate it.

## CONTRITION **LESSON PLAN 1**
### *Trees of sorrow activity*

# CONTRITION **LESSON PLAN 2**
*Prayer before communion bumper sticker activity*

## 12 BLESSING

### Catechist background

There is a very common form of Jewish prayer called *berakhah* (blessing). *Berakhot* (the plural of *berakhah*) are part of the Jewish synagogue services and part of their daily prayers. Berakhot are easy to recognize as they begin with "*barukh*" (in Hebrew, "blessed" or "praised"). The word "*barukh*" is an adjective that describes God as the source of all blessings.

There are three types of *berakhot*: 1) a blessing prayer recited before enjoying a material pleasure such as eating, drinking, or wearing new clothes. This prayer recognizes that God is the Creator of all things; we do not have dominion over things but rather we ask God to use the gifts given to us. 2) a blessing prayer before keeping a commandment. They say this prayer before washing their hands or lighting candles to begin the Sabbath. This helps people be aware that God enables us to do everything we do. 3) a blessing prayer recited at special times and events, such as hearing good or bad news or seeing a beautiful sunset; this prayer reminds the person praying it that God is the ultimate source of all good and evil. What appears to be evil at times is actually a blessing.

### BLESSING LESSON PLAN 1

#### Objectives
- [ ] To be aware of the creation story as a blessing and learn about blessing prayers as one of the five forms of prayer
- [ ] To be aware that God's life in us is a blessing

#### Materials
- [ ] **THE BLESSING SEED,** *A Creation for the New Millennium* by Caitlin Matthews (optional) or use the summary provided
- [ ] **LARGE PIECE OF CONSTRUCTION PAPER**
- [ ] **TREE OF LIFE TEMPLATE** (page 46)
- [ ] **APPLE TEMPLATES** (page 47)
- [ ] **CRAFT STICKS, PETALS, AND FLOWER POTS**

#### The Blessing Seed Summary

*In the middle of Eden was the Tree of Life, and four paths branched out from it. These paths were ways of exploring the world. The first path was called the path of wonder: as the man and woman walked down this path they remembered that they were made from the earth as they heard the birds sing and saw the sun sparkle on the water. The gift of caring was born within them. The second path was called emptiness. On this path they remembered how after they ate the fruit of the Tree of Life, they felt different. The gift of learning was born from times when they felt sad, lonely, or frightened, and when they lost someone they loved. The third path was called the path of making. On this path, the man and woman remembered the song that was inside of them. This path is filled with times when they had good ideas, or made something beautiful. The fourth path was called coming home. On this path, the man and woman remembered that they were a part of everything. They looked after the earth, they spoke for those who had no voice, and they enjoyed and respected all of creation. For the rest of their lives, the gifts of these four paths grew within them as they walked the earth and spread God's blessings everywhere.*

#### Lesson
- Gather the children together.
- Using the background information, introduce the students to the three types of blessing.
- Discuss different practices for each one.
- Read the Blessing Story and discuss it or use the Blessing Seed summary.
- Talk about the many blessings God gave us when the world was created.
- Talk about the four paths, and have

students give examples of experiences they have had related to the four paths.
- Teach the following song:

**Blessings** (Tune: Are You Sleeping)
*Blessing, Blessing*
*Blessing, Blessing*
*Fill our lives, Fill our lives*
*Everywhere a blessing, Everywhere a blessing*
*Look and see, Look and see*

### BLESSING LESSON PLAN 2

**Catechist background**
In the First Book of Chronicles (4:10) in the Bible, we read about a man named Jabez. Jabez's life has a lot to teach us about blessings. First of all, we find that he is more honorable than his brothers. The Bible does not tell us how he achieved this honor, but it does tell us that he prayed for blessing in his life. When he prayed and asked God to bless him, Jabez asked for three things: 1) for more land, 2) for God's hand to be with him, and 3) for God to keep him from harm so he would have no pain. God heard Jabez's prayer and granted his requests. From this man, we learn that no matter what is going on in our lives, we can ask for God's blessing to help us change. God is always with us, protecting us and blessing us with what we need. All we need to do is ask for God's blessing!

**Objectives**
☐ To know God blesses us at all times
☐ To become acquainted with the story of Jabez
☐ To ask God for what we need

**Materials**
☐ **BIBLE**
☐ **HANDS TEMPLATE** (*page 48*)

**Lesson**
- Gather the children and begin the lesson by telling the story of Jabez.
- Discuss what blessings Jabez needed.
- Ask the children to think about the blessings that each of us need.
- Read the quote from Isaiah 41:13, "For I am the Lord, your God, who grasp your right hand; It is I who say to you, 'Fear not, I will help you.'"
- Discuss different ways that God helps us.

## BLESSING **LESSON PLAN 1**
*Tree of life activity*

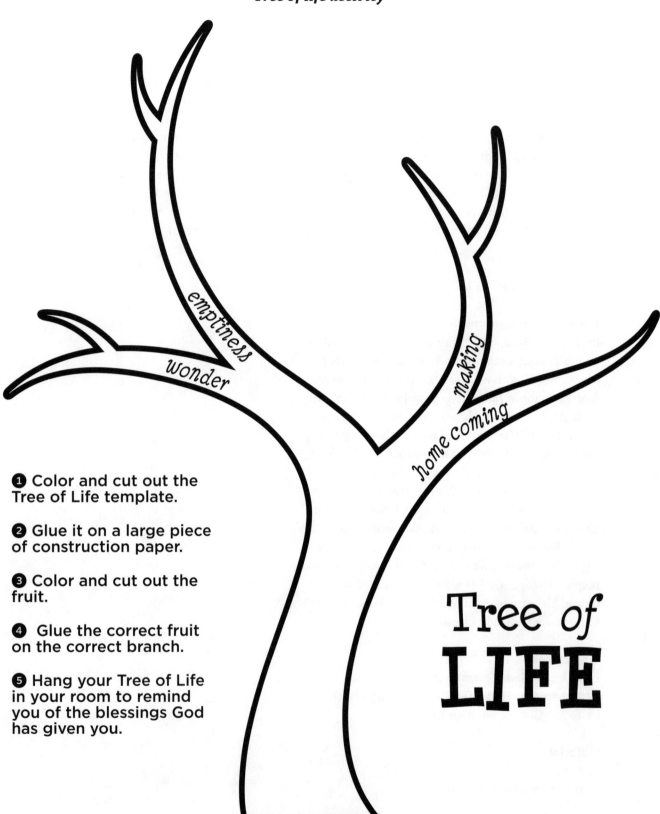

❶ Color and cut out the Tree of Life template.

❷ Glue it on a large piece of construction paper.

❸ Color and cut out the fruit.

❹ Glue the correct fruit on the correct branch.

❺ Hang your Tree of Life in your room to remind you of the blessings God has given you.

# Tree of LIFE

# BLESSING **LESSON PLAN 2**
## *God's hand activity*

Cut out God's Hand template. Trace your hand and forearm. On the tracing of your hand, write blessings that you would like to get from God. Cut out your hand and forearm. Interlock your fingers into God's hand. Put it in your room to remind you God is always with you.

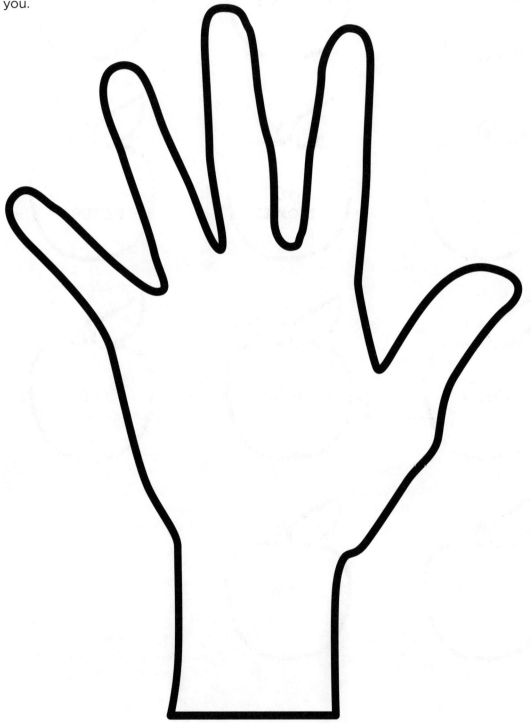

forms of prayer

# 13 PRAISE

**Catechist background**

Praise prayers are easy to teach! We become God's cheerleaders whenever we pray this type of prayer. We get to tell God what a great job God is doing! Many of the psalms found in the Book of Psalms are praise prayers. For example, Psalm 66 reads: "Shout with joy to God, all the earth! Sing the glory of his name; make his praise glorious! Say to God, 'How awesome are your deeds!'" In our own prayer, we might pray "Praise God for the miracle of life" or "Praise God for my best friend." The Glory Be prayer is one of the best "cheers for God."

## PRAISE LESSON PLAN 1

**Objectives**
☐ To discuss what it means to praise God
☐ To write praise prayers

**Materials**
☐ **MARKERS**
☐ **CRAFT STICKS** *to glue flowers on*
☐ **THREE STYROFOAM CUPS**, *per child, for praise bells*
☐ **RIBBON**

**Lesson**
- Gather the children around you. Review the types of prayer: Intercession, Petition, Blessing, Praise, and Thanksgiving.
- Sing the Prayer song found on page 37.
- Focus on Praise prayers. Discuss what it means to praise someone. Ask children to share times when someone has praised them and how they felt. Talk about how God feels when we praise him. Point out that the Gloria at Mass is a praise prayer. Discuss how the Glory Be is also a praise prayer.
- From the previous lesson, get the flower center that says "Praise."
- Get eight previously cut out petals.
- Write a "Praise Prayer" on each of the petals.
- Glue the petals onto the center.
- Glue the flower blossom onto a craft stick and put the craft stick in the flowerpot.
- Proceed with making praise bells.
- Have the children share their praise prayers with the class.
- Sing the Prayer Song.

## Praise bells activity

1. Get three Styrofoam cups.
2. On one cup write "Glory Be to the Father and to the Son and to the Holy Spirit."
3. On the other two cups, write a praise prayer.
4. Punch a hole in the bottom of the cups. Take your ribbon and thread it through.
5. Hang the bells in your room.

## PRAISE LESSON PLAN 2

**Catechist background**

The Book of Psalms is a collection of 150 song-poems. The Psalms were composed over a period of about one thousand years. The Psalms are quoted frequently in the New Testament. The Psalms can be loosely classified according to seven different themes: 1. Praise—extol the nature of God, 2. Historical—focus on the history of the Jewish people, 3. Ethical—focus on human's responsibility, 4. Penitence—focus on human sinfulness, 5. Imprecatory—prayer for the defeat of one's enemies, 6. Messianic—for Christians, Christ has fulfilled these, 7. Ceremonial—focus on Jewish worship rites.

## Objectives
☐ To review praise prayers
☐ To recognize "praise phrases" from the Psalms

## Materials
☐ **Markers**
☐ **Letter to Parents handout**

## Lesson
- Discuss the following quotes:

   *"Yahweh, our Lord, how great your name throughout the earth!"* Psalm 8:1

   *"I will celebrate your love forever, Yahweh."* Psalm 89:1

   *"Yahweh is great, loud must be his praise."* Psalm 96:4

   *"Enter his courts praising him, give thanks to him, bless his name."* Psalm 100:4

- Create a class cheer for God using the word **awesome**. Here is an example:

*Leader:* Give me an A
*Class:* A
*Leader:* A is for Almighty

*Leader:* Give me a W
*Class:* W
*Leader:* W is for Wonderful

*Leader:* Give me an E
*Class:* E
*Leader:* E is for Excellent

*Leader:* Give me an S
*Class:* S
*Leader:* S is for Super

*Leader:* Give me an O
*Class:* O
*Leader:* O is for Outstanding

*Leader:* Give me an M
*Class:* M
*Leader:* M is for Mighty

*Leader:* Give me an E
*Class:* E
*Leader:* E is for Extra Special

*Leader:* What's it spell?
*Class:* Awesome!
*Leader:* Louder
*Class:* Awesome!

- Using the words from your cheer make a Word Chain. Here is an example:

```
                  A
       WONDERFUL
                  M
                  I
                  G
                  H
       OUTSTANDING
                  Y
```

Dear Parent,

We learned how to pray "Praise Prayers." Praise Prayers are simply ways for us to "Cheer God" on!! For example, I might pray "WOW, God, that was a fantastic amount of snow you sent in our last snowstorm." "What a beautiful sunset—the colors are so pretty." Many cheerleaders use megaphones to get the crowd engaged in cheering their team on. Here is a template of a megaphone. Please take time this week to write a family praise prayer on the megaphone. If your child would like to bring the megaphone to class next week, please let him or her do so. We love to share our prayers with each other.

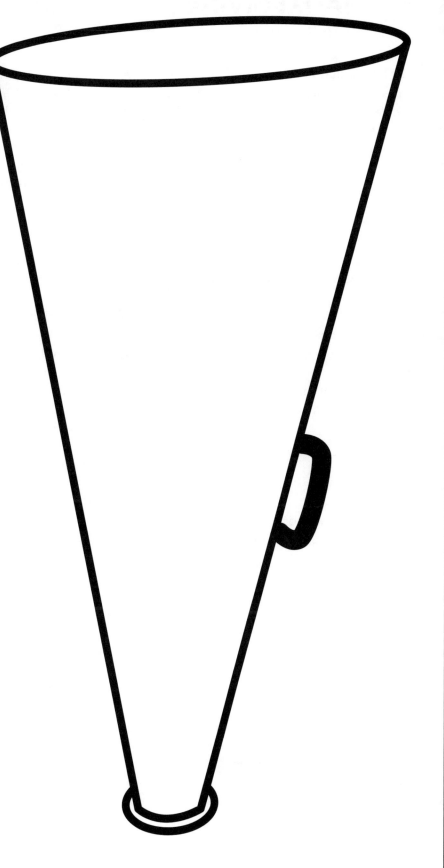

# 14 THANKSGIVING

## Catechist background

Hearts filled with gratitude symbolize this type of prayer. Once we have received what we have asked for, do we take time to thank God for it as well as the many other gifts we have received? Prayers of thanksgiving do not need to be lengthy. Sometimes, it's just a short little prayer, like "Thanks, God, for the beautiful sunset" or "Thanks, God, for the amazing herd of deer I saw in the field."

## THANKSGIVING **LESSON PLAN 1**

### Objectives
- ☐ To introduce examples of thanksgiving prayers
- ☐ To discuss what it means to be filled with gratitude
- ☐ To become aware of the need to say "Thank you" throughout the day

### Materials
- ☐ **3 x 5 cards**
- ☐ **Markers**
- ☐ **Pens**
- ☐ **Lunch-size brown bags**
- ☐ **Paper** *for writing a gratitude acrostic puzzle*

### Lesson
- Gather the children around you. Review the forms of prayer: Intercession, Petition, Blessing, Praise, and Thanksgiving.
- Sing the Prayer Song found on page 37.
- Discuss with students what it means to be thankful. Talk about different things for which they are thankful.
- Ask the students to share times when they have said "Thank you" to someone. Invite them to estimate how many times each day they say "Thank you."
- When do they thank God for all of the gifts that surround us?
- From a previous lesson, get the flower center that says "Gratitude."
- Get eight previously cut out petals.
- Write a prayer of gratitude on each petal.
- Glue the petals onto the center.
- Glue the flower blossom onto a craft stick and put the craft stick in the flowerpot.
- Continue with the acrostic activity.
- Sing the Prayer Song

## Gratitude acrostic activity

**❶** Think of something for which you are very thankful.

**❷** Write the letters of the word down the side of your paper.

**❸** Using words that start with each of those letters, explain the object, how you feel about it, why it's important to you, and what life would be like without it.

**❹** Decorate your acrostic puzzle.

Here is a sample:

**F** *un to be with, teasing, laughing, happy and sad*

**A** *lways looking out for each other*

**M** *eals on the run or picnics in the park*

**I** *nside or outside, we like to be together*

**L** *ove is all around us*

**Y** *ou, me, siblings, and caretakers*

### THANKSGIVING **LESSON PLAN 2**

**Catechist background**

There are several biblical references that focus on gratitude. One is found in Luke 17:11–19. Jesus heals the lepers and asks them to show themselves to the priests. Only one returns to give thanks. Another reference is Daniel 2:23. Daniel thanks God for giving him wisdom and power. St. Paul tells the Thessalonians to be thankful for everything (1 Thessalonians 5:18).

**Objectives**
- ☐ To review prayers of thanksgiving
- ☐ To create a litany of thanks
- ☐ To know different scriptural references that focus on thanksgiving

**Materials**
- ☐ **Variety of old magazines**
- ☐ **Brown paper lunch bags**
- ☐ **3 x 5 cards**

**Lesson**
- Gather students around you.
- Review what it means to be thankful.
- Share any of the Scripture references above and discuss with the students.
- Play soft music and tell children they are going to look for pictures in magazines of things they are thankful for. Each child should find five pictures and cut them out. Children will do this without talking. (Note: If time is limited, reduce the number of pictures to three.)
- After everyone has their pictures, gather in a circle. Begin by explaining that you are going to pray a litany of thanks. Each person will hold up one picture and say, " I am thankful for _____," and the rest of the class responds, "Thanks, God." Go around the entire circle until all of the pictures are shared.
- After you finish the litany, explain to students that you are going to start a project that they will continue at home with their parents.
- Give each student five 3 x 5 cards. On each card, have the student draw a picture and write either the word or a sentence about what they are thankful for.
- On the brown paper bag, the child writes his or her name and the following phrase: "[Name's] Gratitude Grab Bag."
- Have the child put the cards in his or her bag.
- Give each child seven blank cards to take home. Each evening for a week, the family can create a new card and put it in the bag.
- Determine a date for all children to bring their bags back to class.
- Predetermine which children are going to exchange bags. The child takes home a classmate's bag. Each evening, the family pulls out one card and says a thank you prayer based on what is on the card.

# PARENT LETTER FOR GRATITUDE GRAB BAGS

Dear parent,

Your child is learning about various forms of prayer. During our time together, we discussed what it means to be grateful. As a class, we decided that our lives are filled with many moments of gratitude. We are grateful for small things like puppies and flowers. We are grateful for all the people who love us, especially friends and family.

We would like you to join us in a special project. Each child has brought home a Gratitude Grab Bag. Over the next 7 days, please take a few moments each day to talk about one thing that your entire family is grateful for. Let your child draw the picture and help him or her to write a word or a sentence describing the picture. Please have your child bring the Gratitude Grab Bag back to class on _____. During this class, students will exchange bags. Your child will bring home another child's Gratitude Grab Bag. Each evening, please pull out one of the cards and as a family say a prayer of gratitude not only for the object that was pulled out but also for the family whose bag you have.

# 15 IMAGINATIVE PRAYERS

*meditative prayer*

Teaching young children to meditate is simple if done in small steps. The first step is to get children comfortable with short periods of silence. One way to do this is to introduce students to a new classmate, "Pat Penguin." Pat can be a drawing or a stuffed animal. Whenever the penguin is present, everyone is going to be very quiet. Dim the classroom lights, put on soft music, and ask children to lie down. Invite them to listen for the sounds around them. What classroom noises do they hear? What people noises do they hear? Ask them to breathe deeply and begin to relax. This simple exercise needs to be done four or five times or until you sense the children are comfortable with this routine. The second step is to give each child a "prayer mat." Inexpensive place mats make wonderful prayer mats. Explain to the students that whenever we get ready to pray in a very special way, we will use our prayer mats and Pat Penguin will be with us.

## IMAGINATIVE PRAYER LESSON PLAN 1

**Catechist background**

We live in a very rational, systematic world. Many of us make to-do lists. There's a sense of accomplishment as we finish jobs and cross them off the list. We move quickly from one task to another. Deep within us, our souls long for stories in which we can identify with the characters as they experience despair and hope, cowardice and courage, hate and love. Our minds are filled with images, sounds, smells, and memories that God uses to open our hearts. Praying with our imaginations allows us to take familiar Scripture stories and let them flow through our hearts.

St. Ignatius Loyola used the imagination to help people know and love God. Imaginative prayer is at the heart of the Spiritual Exercises that he developed. Ignatius presents two different ways of imagining in the Spiritual Exercises. The first way is to "enter into the vision of God." During this prayer experience, Ignatius asks us to put ourselves in God's place and look at our world filled with natural disasters, with people who make good choices and not so good choices, and feel the concern God has for our world. When praying, we try to see everything from God's perspective and take on God's qualities of love, gentleness, compassion, understanding, and patience.

**Objectives**
☐ To see the world through God's eyes

**Materials**
☐ **AMY GRANT'S SONG "MY FATHER'S EYES"** *(optional)*
☐ **WHITE DRAWING PAPER**
☐ **CRAYONS**
☐ **MARKERS**

**Lesson**
- Gather the students around you and begin to discuss what it means to imagine or pretend. Talk about things students like to imagine or pretend.
- Discuss what it means to look at something through another person's eyes. For example, if one is a teacher and one of the teacher's students gets an A, how do you think the teacher feels? Why? If one is a fireman and goes to put a fire out at someone's house, how do you think the fireman feels? How does the person whose house is burning feel?
- Let's pretend you are God and you are looking at the earth from heaven. What do you see? How does it make you feel?
- Discuss how some people can see the good in someone when other

people can't, and give examples.
- If desired, play the song "My Father's Eyes," and talk about the meaning of the song.
- Continue with God's Feelings activity *(page 57)*.
- Invite children to share their pictures with the class.

## IMAGINATIVE PRAYER **LESSON PLAN 2**

### Catechist background

The second way to experience imaginative prayer is to place one's self within a Bible story. Using our imagination, we can either be an onlooker or a participant in the story. In Luke 5:18–26 we read the story of the paralytic on the mat. "Some men came along carrying a paralytic on a mat." *I can imagine that I am the paralyzed man on the mat. What does it feel like not to be able to move? What do I miss doing? What is the color of my mat?* "They were trying to bring him in and lay him before Jesus, but they found no way of getting him through because of the crowd, so they went up on the roof." *Why do I want my friends to take me to Jesus? What are the names of my friends who carry me to Jesus? How do I feel knowing that I want to ask Jesus to heal me? When I get to the house and see all of those people, do I want to give up?* "There they let him down with his mat through the tiles into the middle of the crowd before Jesus." *How do my friends get through the roof? When I'm being lowered down, do I feel embarrassed? Do I almost fall off my mat? How does Jesus look? What is he wearing? What does he say to me? What does he say to my friends?* "Seeing their faith, Jesus said, 'My friend, your sins are forgiven you.'" *How do I feel when Jesus calls me a friend? How do the friends who brought me here act? Are they happy when Jesus calls me a friend?* "Jesus addressed the paralyzed man: 'I say to you, get up! Take your mat with you and return to your house.' At once the man stood up before them. He picked up the mat he had been lying on and went home praising God." *When Jesus tells me to get up, am I afraid? Do my legs feel shaky? Are the people who are watching smiling? Where are my friends? As soon as I stand up, what do I do? Do I run and thank my friends? Do I thank Jesus? Do I walk home to tell my family? What will I remember most about that day?*

Once again, you will want to set a quiet atmosphere with low lights and soft music. Bring out Pat Penguin and the prayer mats before you begin this prayer experience. You can use any Bible story that you like. You may want to write questions out ahead of time. Or as you become more proficient, slowly read the story and ask questions that come to mind as you read. Be sure to pause after each question. Afterward, share what you and the children imagined as you prayed.

### Objectives
☐ To pray using one's imagination

### Materials
☐ **Soft music**
☐ **Pat Penguin**
☐ **Prayer Mats**
☐ **Bible Story**

### Lesson
- Gather the children around you.
- Prepare a silent, prayerful atmosphere. Get out Pat Penguin and the prayer mats, and put on soft music.
- Using the background material, slowly read Luke 5:18–26, asking questions as you read. Allow plenty of time for children to respond silently.
- After the last question, allow children to remain still for several minutes.
- Gather children in a circle and allow them to share what they saw, heard, and felt as you guided them through this prayer experience.

# IMAGINATIVE PRAYER **LESSON PLAN 1**
## *God's feelings activity*

Take a sheet of paper and fold it in half. Fold it in half again. Open it up—there are four boxes. In the first box, write "God is happy because_____." Draw a picture of what makes God happy. In the second box, write "God cries because_____." Draw a picture of what makes God cry. In the third box, write "God laughs because_____." Draw a picture of what makes God laugh. In the fourth box, write "God is angry because_____." Draw a picture of what makes God angry.

| God is happy because | God cries because |
|---|---|
| God laughs because | God is angry because |

# IMAGINATIVE PRAYER **LESSON PLAN 2**
## *Imaginative prayer activity: Matthew 4:18–21*

Dear Parent,

Today, your child learned how to use his or her imagination while praying. Below is a short imaginative prayer experience you can use with your child before bedtime. Please take a few minutes and help your child quiet down before beginning. Your child knows how to relax and get ready to pray. Feel free to put soft music on in the background. Then read the Bible story slowly, pausing for a few minutes after each question. Give your child time to imagine the answer. I encourage you to also imagine the scene as you lead your child through this prayer. At the end, share with each other what you imagined and felt. I hope this experience will bring your family closer to God, who loves you so much.

"As Jesus was walking along the Sea of Galilee he watched two brothers, Simon now known as Peter and his brother Andrew, casting a net into the sea. *What is Jesus wearing? What color are his clothes? Does he look happy? What does he see as he walks along the beach? What are Peter and Andrew wearing? Is it a hot day? Do Peter and Andrew look happy? What kind of net do they have? Is it large or small? What are they trying to catch?* "They were fishermen. Jesus said to them, 'Come after me and I will make you fishers of men.' They immediately left their nets and became his followers." *Why does Jesus want Andrew and Peter to follow him? How do the brothers feel? Do they want to follow Jesus? What does it mean to be a fisher of men? Is it easy to follow Jesus? What makes it hard to follow Jesus?* "He walked along farther and caught sight of two other brothers, James, Zebedee's son, and his brother John. They too were in their boat getting their nets in order with their father, Zebedee." *What are James and John wearing? What are they doing? What kind of boat do they have? Is it a rowboat? A canoe? A sailboat? What color is it? Are they surprised when they see Jesus? Do they know Andrew and Peter? Do they call hello to their friends? Are they getting ready to fish?* "Jesus called them, and immediately they left the boat and their father to follow Jesus." *Why would they leave their father? Were they excited to follow Jesus? Are you excited to follow Jesus? What are different ways that you can follow Jesus?*

#  LECTIO DIVINA

**Catechist background**

*Lectio divina* means "holy reading" and refers to a method of meditative Scripture reading practiced by monastics in the early church. St. Benedict is usually associated with this practice, but it was an 11th-century Carthusian monk named Guigo who formalized the method in a letter he wrote to a friend. This letter is known as the "Stairway to Heaven" and describes a four-rung ladder to heaven. Each rung is one of the four steps of the method mentioned in lesson plan one.

## LECTIO DIVINA **LESSON PLAN 1**

**Objectives**
- ☐ To teach students to use the *lectio divina* form of meditation

**Materials**
- ☐ PAT PRAYER PENGUIN
- ☐ PLACE MATS *one for each child to sit on (prayer mat)*
- ☐ CHILDREN'S BIBLE
- ☐ SOFT MUSIC

**Lesson**
- ■ Gather the children around you.
- ■ Using the background material for catechists, begin introducing children to *lectio divina*.
- ■ Introduce *lectio divina* in small incremental steps.
- ■ Explain that lectio divina is a four-step process.
- ■ Tell the students we will always begin our special prayer called *lectio divina*, which means "holy reading," by putting our prayer mat on the floor and lying down on it so it is underneath our shoulders. Following are the four steps of this method. We will begin with Step 1.

1. Read a short Scripture passage. Give the students a brief idea of the passage. For example, today I'm going to read you the story of the prodigal son. Read Luke 15:11-24.

2. Tell the children you are going to read the same passage again very slowly. Ask them to listen for a word or a phrase that makes them think about God or a word or a phrase that makes them think about how this passage connects to them. For example, in the story of the prodigal son, I might think about someone I need to forgive. Read the Scripture passage very slowly.

3. After thinking about the Scripture passage, think about an action the Scripture is calling you to do. For example, do I need to call my friend and apologize? Do I need to pray for someone? Do I need to be a better friend to someone?

4. Now, it's time to just be in God's presence. Lie quietly and listen for God's voice in your heart.

- • Tell the students that if they are doing this at home in their rooms, this is the end of the prayer. However, if you do it as a class, there is a step five: we sit in a circle and share the word or phrases that were special to us and the action we are going to do. Students tend to be very open. It's amazing what they hear God tell them!
- • Be sure to "think aloud" during each step until students become familiar with the process.
- • Continue the lesson by explaining the *lectio divina* activity.

**NOTE:** It's very important to do this prayer process in small steps. In the beginning, do steps one and two for several weeks before adding step three and then step four. Choosing the right Scripture passage is very important. Choose one that is familiar to your students and age-level appropriate. You may prefer to use a children's Bible. In the beginning, try to get them to "meditate" for 10 minutes. By the end of the year, see if they can meditate for thirty minutes.

## LECTIO DIVINA **LESSON PLAN 2**

### Objectives
☐ To practice *lectio divina*

### Materials
☐ **CHILDREN'S BIBLE**
☐ **SOFT MUSIC**
☐ **PAT PRAYER PENGUIN**
☐ **PRAYER MAT**

### Lesson
- Gather the children around you.
- Review the purpose of Pat Prayer Penguin and prayer mats.
- Choose an appropriate Scripture. Here are some suggestions: Matthew 8:5–13; Matthew 13:44–46; Mark 10:13–16; Mark 12:41–44.
- Using lesson plan one, meditate with the *lectio divina* process.

## LECTIO DIVINA **LESSON PLAN 1**
### *Lectio Divina take home activity*

Dear Parents,

Today, our class began learning how to meditate. A new classmate joined us, Pat Prayer Penguin. Whenever Pat Prayer Penguin is present, the children know they will have a very special silent prayer experience. Each child has a special prayer mat to remind him or her that we are preparing to listen to God in a very special way. I've listed below the four-step process of Lectio Divina so that if you and your child want to try this at home you are able to do so. I also wanted to let you know about this special prayer so if your child talks about it, you will be able to respond. I encourage you to try this with your child just before bedtime. It's a very special way to pray!

Sincerely,

## HERE IS THE FOUR-STEP PROCESS:

**Step one:** The teacher will read a short Scripture passage. Give students a brief idea of the passage. For example, "Today I'm going to read you the story of the prodigal son." Read the passage.

**Step two:** Tell the children you are going to read the same passage again very slowly. Ask them to listen for a word or a phrase that makes them think about God, or a word or a phrase that makes them think about how this story connects to them. For example, in the story of the prodigal son, I might think about someone I need to forgive. Read the Scripture passage very slowly.

**Step three:** After thinking about the Scripture passage, think about an action the Scripture is calling you to do. For example, do I need to call my friend and apologize? Do I need to pray for someone? Do I need to be a better friend to someone?

**Step Four:** Now, it's time to just be in God's presence. I need to lie quietly and listen for God's voice in my heart.

# LECTIO DIVINA **LESSON PLAN 2**
*Lectio Divina ladder activity*

Stay quiet and listen to God's voice.

Think of an action to do that connects with the word.

Reread the Bible story slowly. Choose a word to think about.

Read the Bible story.

# meditative prayer

## 17 ART AS PRAYER

**Catechist background**

There are two different ways of using art for prayer. The first way is by observing the artwork of another. As one looks at a stained-glass window or any piece of art, the experience has the power to change us from within as we connect what we see to our experience of God. It is quite possible that in quiet gazing upon the artwork one might become aware of a new gift God is giving at that moment.

Here are some easy steps to prepare for this type of prayer experience with children.

1. Become very quiet; breathe deeply and slowly; become aware of the quiet within.
2. Spend a couple of minutes silently thanking God for the gifts of this day.
3. Look very carefully at the picture. Is there a figure, shape, color, or texture that stands out to you? What is it saying?
4. What feelings, thoughts, or ideas do you have? What do they tell you about God?
5. Share with God what you find important as you look at the picture.
6. Thank God for this opportunity to spend time with God.

The very first time you introduce this to your students, you need to model it for them. Think aloud each step, and share what you are experiencing. It won't take them long to join in with you. After you do one together, then you can move to a silent group experience.

### ART AS PRAYER LESSON PLAN 1

**Objectives**
☐ To experience an artist's work as prayer

**Materials**
☐ **AN ART IMAGE** (*portraits, scenes, sculpture, etc.*)

**Lesson**
- Gather the children around you.
- Display an art image.
- Instruct the children to become very quiet and become aware of their breathing; wait until your class is quiet and focused.
- Ask your class to silently thank God for gifts they see around them.
- Tell your students to look at the picture on page 68. Ask them how it reminds them of God.
- You might share that God is like a mother polar bear always taking care of us or God is gentle like a mother polar bear or God likes to play like the little bear cubs.
- Ask students to talk to God about the image. "Thanks, God, for always taking care of me and for teaching me how to be gentle and kind. Thanks, God, for giving me someone to take care of me. Help me to take care of my friends when they need me."
- Ask children to talk to God about how they like to spend time with God.
- Explain the take home activity and end the lesson with prayer.

## ART AS PRAYER LESSON PLAN 2

### Catechist background

Another way to pray using art is to create your own art. A person doesn't have to be "good at art" in order to have this experience. Many artists see themselves as collaborating with creation. Some artists work in silence as they prepare their material. They tune in to how they feel. They listen to the silence to hear how they are going to begin their art. Sometimes in the middle of the process, the artist stops and asks for God's help as he or she considers how to continue the work. Most artists do not understand where their work comes from, but are aware that they participated in a silent, sacred process that brought out a new image.

### Objectives
☐ To pray using scribble drawings that the students will create

### Materials
☐ **11" x 17" WHITE PAPER**, *one for each child*
☐ **CRAYONS**
☐ **MARKERS**

### Lesson
- Gather the students around you.
- Put on soft music and let students know they will work in silence.
- Explain that using our creativity is a prayer.
- Tell them to ask God to be with them as they draw and color.
- Continue the lesson with the Scribble Drawing and Story activity.
- When the activity is finished, have some of the children share some of their creations.
- End with a few moments of silent prayer.

### Scribble drawing and story activity

❶ Take a large sheet of paper and choose your favorite colored marker.

❷ Put the marker in the hand you do not write with. Close your eyes and pretend your hand is dancing across the paper making lines, circles, loops, etc. Don't be afraid if you go off the paper. Just put your hand back on and continue. When you feel you have finished, lay your marker down and open your eyes.

❸ Get different colored markers. Look at your paper; can you see different objects in your drawing? For example, you might see a hat—outline the hat and decorate it; you also might see a duck—do the same thing: outline it and decorate it. Rotate your paper in all directions and look for other objects; outline and decorate.

❹ Write a story that uses all of the objects you found.

❺ Share your picture and story with a friend.

# ART AS PRAYER **LESSON PLAN 1**
## *Take home activity*

Dear Parents,

Today, our class learned how to pray using an art image. Below, you will find the steps for the prayer experience as well as an art image. Please encourage your child to teach you how to pray this way. If you have any questions, please contact me. I look forward to hearing from you about this experience.
Thank you.

**ART PRAYER EXPERIENCE STEPS**

1. Become very quiet; breathe deeply; slowly become aware of the quiet within.

2. Spend a couple of minutes silently thanking God for the gifts of this day.

3. Look very carefully at the picture. Is there a figure, shape, color, or texture that stands out to you?

4. What feelings, thoughts, or desires do you notice? What do they tell you about God?

5. Share with God what you find important as you look at the picture.

6. Thank God for this opportunity to spend time with God.

**ART IMAGES**
Let your child choose which image most appeals to him or her.

# Answer Crossword puzzle activity [ page 12 ]

## OUR FATHER LESSON PLAN 1
*Crossword puzzle activity*

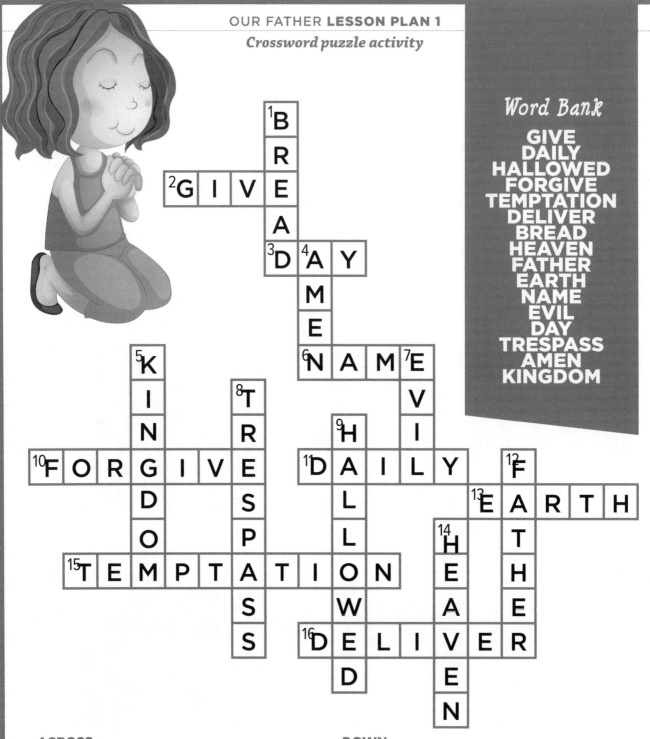

**Word Bank**
GIVE
DAILY
HALLOWED
FORGIVE
TEMPTATION
DELIVER
BREAD
HEAVEN
FATHER
EARTH
NAME
EVIL
DAY
TRESPASS
AMEN
KINGDOM

**ACROSS**
2. To offer something to another person
3. A period of 24 hours
6. A person's identification
10. To show mercy
11. To do something every day
13. The planet we live on
15. The desire to do something wrong
16. To hand over

**DOWN**
1. Food made of flour, water, and yeast
4. Word said at the end of a prayer
5. The spiritual domain
7. Very bad
8. To enter someplace without permission
9. To honor as holy
12. Creator of heaven and earth
14. The home of God and the angels

# Answer Word search activity [ page 20 ]

**HAIL MARY LESSON PLAN 1**
*Word search activity*

# Hail Mary

Find the following words in the word search. There will be eight letters that are not circled. Unscramble the eight letters to find the mystery words. Words can be found horizontally, vertically, diagonally, backwards and forwards.

- AMONG
- FRUIT
- LORD
- SINNERS
- BLEST
- GRACE
- MOTHER
- WOMB
- DEATH
- JESUS
- PRAY
- WOMEN

| E | P | R | A | Y | M | S | H |
|---|---|---|---|---|---|---|---|
| C | H | L | M | O | U | A | N |
| A | T | R | T | S | B | E | D |
| R | A | H | E | B | M | F | R |
| G | E | J | L | O | O | R | O |
| R | D | E | W | I | W | U | L |
| Y | S | R | E | N | N | I | S |
| T | A | M | O | N | G | T | A |

Mystery words:

# HAIL
# MARY

# My favorite prayers

# Also Available

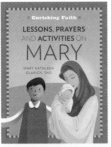

*Enriching Faith*
**LESSONS, PRAYERS AND ACTIVITIES ON MARY**

MARY KATHLEEN GLAVICH, SND

Help children develop a lifelong love for our Blessed Mother with these kid-friendly lessons and activities. Each lesson is reinforced with engaging activity sheets, plus background information for catechists and teachers.

72 PAGES | $14.95 | 9781627851459

*Enriching Faith*
**LESSONS, PRAYERS AND ACTIVITIES ON THE TEACHINGS OF JESUS**

LEE DANESCO

Use this creative and engaging activity book to help you teach children in first grade and beyond about Jesus' teachings on loving God and neighbor.

72 PAGES | $14.95 | 9781627851046

*Enriching Faith*
**PRAYERS AND ACTIVITIES ON SERVICE**

PATRICIA MATHSON

Help children make Christian service a way of life with this creative collection of outreach projects, learning experiences, and prayers.

72 PAGES | $14.95 | 9781585959372

*Enriching Faith*
**LESSONS AND ACTIVITIES ON THE BIBLE**

MARY KATHLEEN GLAVICH, SND

Here are creative ways to introduce biblical lands and cultures, versions of the Bible, biblicalreference tools, and techniques for using Scripture as a basis for prayer.

72 PAGES | $14.95 | 9781627850278

*Enriching Faith*
**LESSONS AND ACTIVITIES ON PRAYER**

CATHERINE STEWART

Here are dozens of fresh ideas to help your students see prayer in a whole new light.

72 PAGES | $14.95 | 9781585959471

**TO ORDER CALL 1-800-321-0411**
OR VISIT WWW.TWENTYTHIRDPUBLICATIONS.COM

**TWENTY-THIRD PUBLICATIONS**